RULES OF THE GAME

This game is probably best played with other people, so if you can, play it with friends or family.

If you have two players

- Player 1 takes the book and asks the player two a question beginning with the phrase, "Would you rather...? Why?"
- After player 2 has made his/her choice, he/she has to explain the reason why the choice was made.
- Pass the book to the other player, and they ask you a question.
- Learn lots about one another, have fun, and giggles.
- The two-player game version could work well as an ice-breaker exercise before introductions in classes or meetings

If you have three or four players

- Out of your group, decide who will be the Question Master. If you can't decide, have folded bits of paper with 'Question Master' written on one, and 'players' on the other, and each pick one.
- The Question Master asks one question from the book.
- The other two or three people give their answers.
- The Question Master decides who has given the best answer - this is the answer with the best explanation for why. The explanations can be funny or creative or well thought out. The Question Master's decision is final. One point is given for the best answer. If the Question Master can't decide, both players get one point each.
- The first player to reach a score of 10 points wins.

--- LET THE FUN BEGIN ---

WOULD YOU RATHER......

Eat a popsicle

-OR-

eat a cupcake

WOULD YOU RATHER......

Be a doctor

a pilot

WOULD YOU RATHER...

Raise
a cat **or** a dog

WOULD YOU RATHER......

Be a master
at drawing

-OR-

Be amazing
at singing

WOULD YOU RATHER......

Sail
a boat

-OR-

ride
in a hang

WOULD YOU RATHER...

Live

in the jungle **or** near the sea

WOULD YOU RATHER......

be able to

control fire

-OR-

water

WOULD YOU RATHER......

Meet your favorite celebrity

-*OR*-

be on a TV show

WOULD YOU YOU RATHER...

<u>Dance</u> **or** <u>sing</u>
in front of
1000 people

WOULD YOU RATHER......

Have super strength

-OR-

Be invisible

WOULD YOU RATHER......

Live in the suburbs

-OR-

live in the city

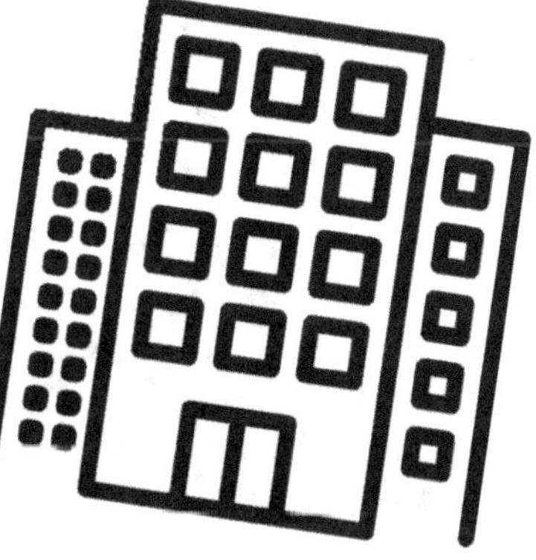

WOULD YOU RATHER......

Go to a water-park

-OR-

go skiing

WOULD YOU RATHER...

It be

<u>*raining*</u> **or** <u>*snowing*</u>

WOULD YOU RATHER......

Be a fast swimmer

-OR-

a fast runner

WOULD YOU RATHER......

Ride a big horse

-OR-

a small pony

WOULD YOU RATHER......

Have 3 arms

-OR-

have only 1 leg

WOULD YOU RATHER...

Kiss a frog **_or_** Hug a snake

WOULD YOU RATHER...

it be really hot **_or_** *really cold*

WOULD YOU RATHER......

Lie to your parents 

-OR-

lie to your friends 

WOULD YOU RATHER......

Be a
scientist

-OR-

a boss of
a company

WOULD YOU RATHER......

have a penguin

-OR-

a Komodo dragon...

as a pet?

WOULD YOU RATHER...

not use compu-
ter

or

not
eat
junk
food

for a month?

WOULD YOU RATHER.......

It be Christmas

-OR-

your birthday

everyday?

WOULD YOU RATHER......

live in Narnia

-OR-

go to Hogwarts

WOULD YOU RATHER......

swim with dolphins 

-OR-

 fly with birds

WOULD YOU YOU

RATHER...

have a   a huge

tree **or** trampo

house   -line

WOULD YOU RATHER......

Be very tall Be very short

-OR-

WOULD YOU RATHER......

have long
hair

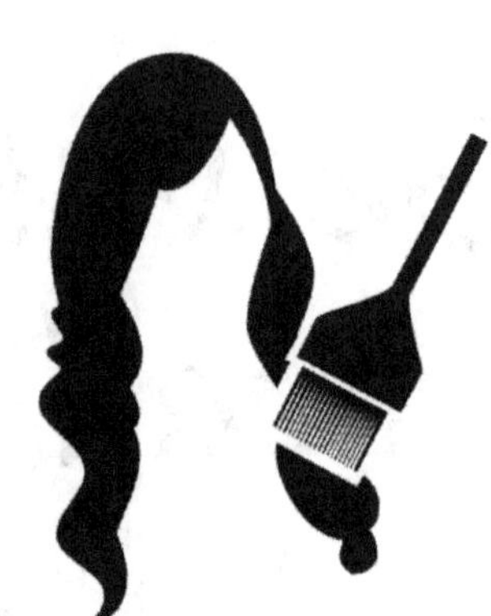

-OR-

have short
hair

WOULD YOU RATHER......

have a submarine 

-OR-

a space shuttle

WOULD YOU RATHER......

take a day trip to

the
zoo
-OR-
the
beach

WOULD YOU RATHER......

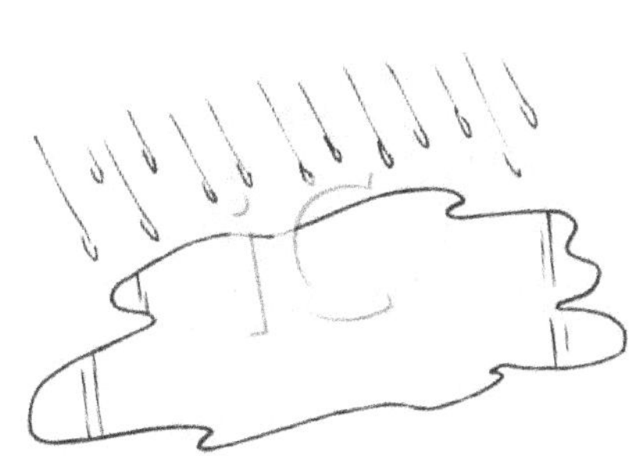

play in a mud puddle

-OR-

a pool

WOULD YOU RATHER......

wear a
suit

-OR-

casual
clothes
everyday?

WOULD YOU RATHER......

Eat cookies

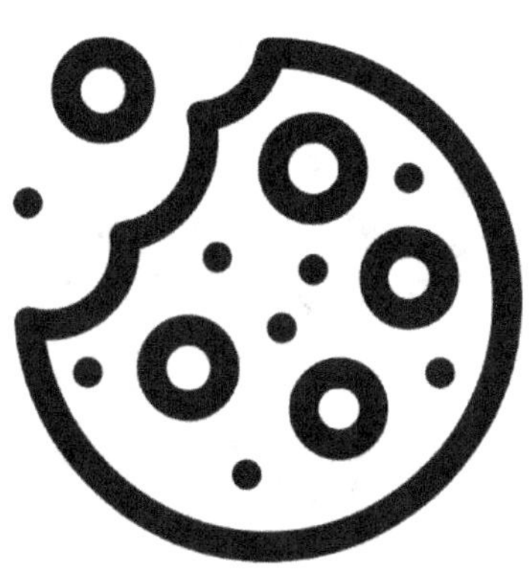

-OR-

have a cake

WOULD YOU RATHER......

Play video games

play outside

WOULD YOU RATHER......

Be a
wizard

-OR-

be a
superhero

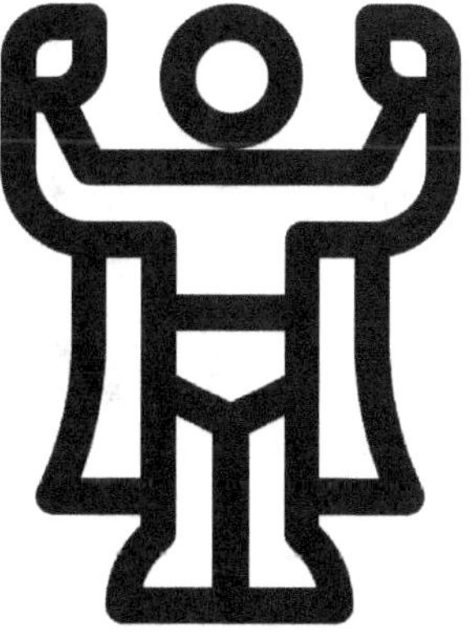

WOULD YOU RATHER......

Go diving

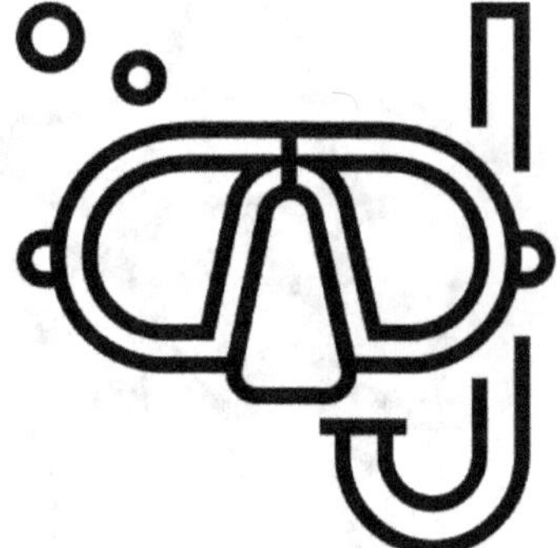

-OR-

Camp by a lake

WOULD YOU RATHER......

have any book you wanted

-OR-

Watch any movie you wanted

WOULD YOU RATHER......

Ride a roller coaster

-OR-

Go down a giant water slide

WOULD YOU RATHER......

Play
soccer

-OR-

Play
baseball

WOULD YOU RATHER......

Fly a kite 

-OR-

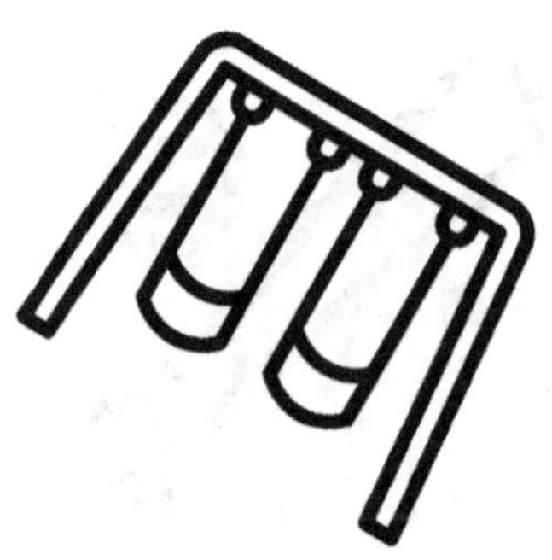

Swing on a swing

WOULD YOU RATHER......

Be
incredibly
funny

-OR-

Be

incredibly

smart

WOULD YOU RATHER......

Spend the whole day in

A museum **or** _a garden_

WOULD YOU RATHER......

eat a hamburger 

eat a hot dog

WOULD YOU RATHER......

Be an amazing writer

-OR-

An amazing photographer

WOULD YOU RATHER......

Have 10 mosquito bites

-OR-

One bee sting

WOULD YOU RATHER......

Ride a skate board

-OR-

A bike

WOULD YOU RATHER……

Go sky diving

-OR-

Go climbing

WOULD YOU RATHER......

Ride a
camel

-OR-

Ride a
unicorn

WOULD YOU RATHER......

have pancake
for dinner

-OR-

pizza for
breakfast

for a year?

WOULD YOU RATHER......

Be able
to fly

-OR-

Be able to
turn anything
into gold

WOULD YOU RATHER......

Have pancake
for dinner

-OR-

Have pizza
for
breakfast

WOULD YOU RATHER......

Be a policeman

-OR-

A fire fighter

WOULD YOU RATHER......

Swim in chocolate

-OR-

Swim in popcorn

WOULD YOU RATHER......

Have no homework

-OR-

Have no tests

WOULD YOU RATHER......

Learn to surf

-OR-

Learn to skate

WOULD YOU RATHER......

Have 100$ -OR- 1000$ in a now year

WOULD YOU RATHER......

Drink

Orange juice **-OR-** Milk

WOULD YOU RATHER......

Be able to
read minds

-OR-

See the
future

WOULD YOU RATHER......

Drive your own car

-OR-

Have the car drive itself

WOULD YOU RATHER......

own the strongest

computer

-OR-

phone

WOULD YOU RATHER......

Go to a bookstore

Go to a party

WOULD YOU RATHER......

drink a cup of

Coffee   Tea

-OR-

WOULD YOU RATHER......

get a new pair of shoes

-OR-

A new t-shirt

WOULD YOU RATHER......

drive a race car 

-OR-

fly a helicopter 

WOULD YOU RATHER......

Travel by train

Travel by plane

WOULD YOU RATHER......

eat a dead bug

-OR-

eat an alive worm

WOULD YOU RATHER......

Get up
very early

Stay up
very late

WOULD YOU RATHER......

Go to the gym

-OR-

Go to the cinema

WOULD YOU RATHER......

have a ten dollar bill 

-OR-

ten dollars in coins 

WOULD YOU RATHER......

eat out at a restaurant

-OR-

have a homemade meal

WOULD YOU RATHER......

Have one more

Hand -OR- Foot

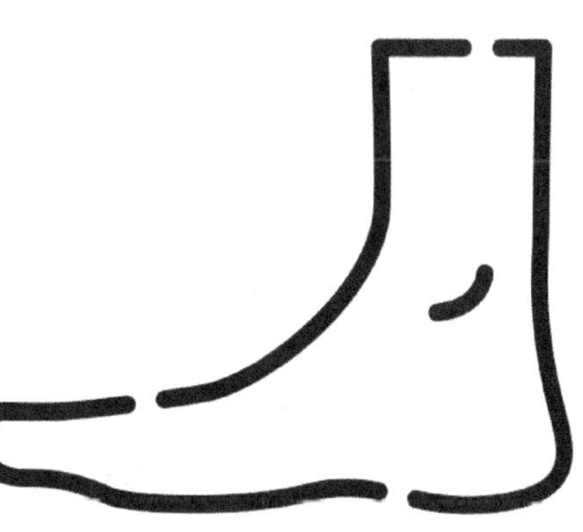

WOULD YOU RATHER......

Live in a castle

-OR-

Live in a space station

WOULD YOU RATHER......

have a bowl of

Noodles   Rice

-OR-

WOULD YOU RATHER......

Be really good at math

-OR-

be really good at sports

WOULD YOU RATHER......

Eat a
whole

<u>lemon</u> *or* <u>onion</u>

WOULD YOU RATHER......

Take a
coding
class

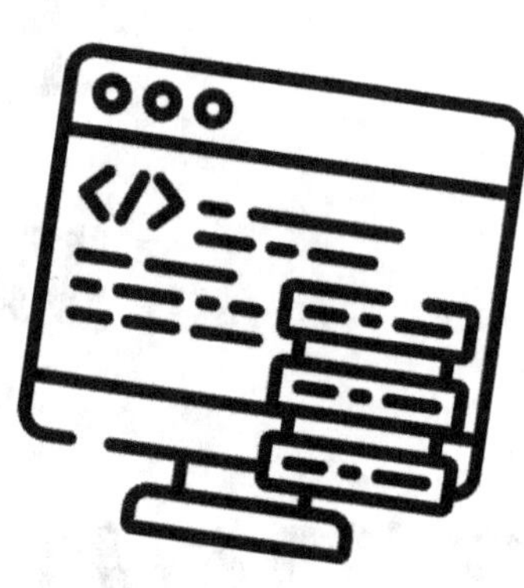

-OR-

An art
class

WOULD YOU RATHER......

have your own private movie theater

-OR-

private arcade

WOULD YOU RATHER......

be stranded on a desert island

-OR-

in the forest

WOULD YOU RATHER......

own a mouse -sized elephant

-OR-

a elephant -sized mouse

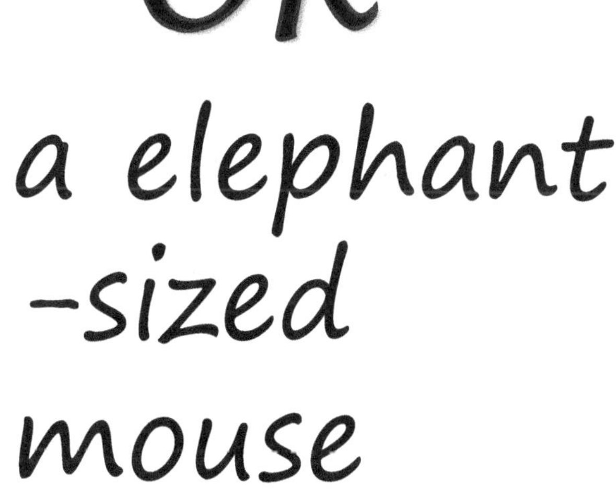

WOULD YOU RATHER......

Have 3 free wishes

-OR-

be the richest man

WOULD YOU RATHER......

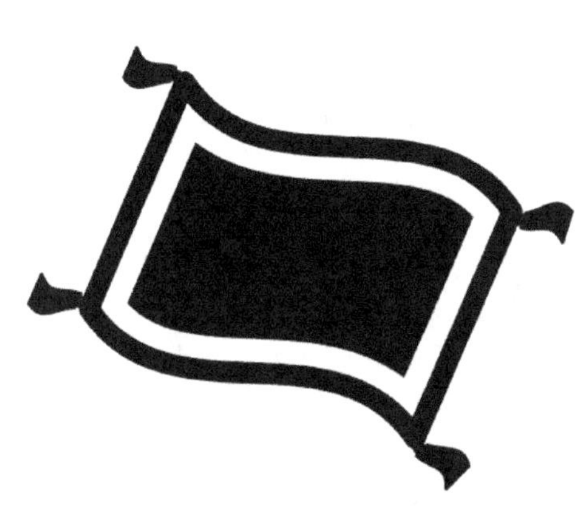

have a magic carpet

-OR-

your own personal robot

WOULD YOU RATHER......

Be able to do flips

-OR-

Break dance

WOULD YOU RATHER......

Be able to walk on all fours

-OR-

Only be able to walk sideways

WOULD YOU RATHER......

Live in a house shaped like a <u>circle</u> **or** <u>triangle</u>

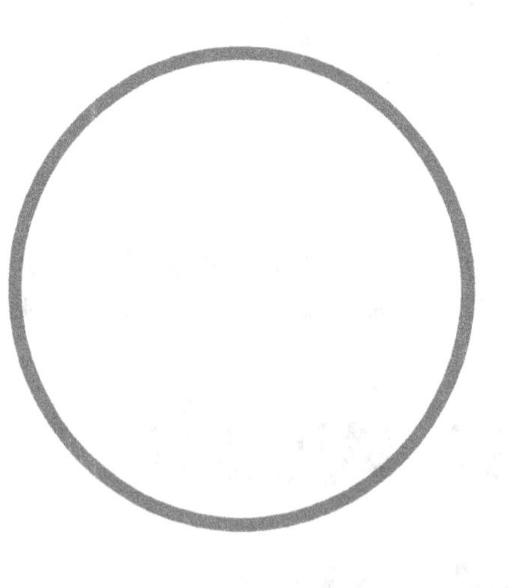 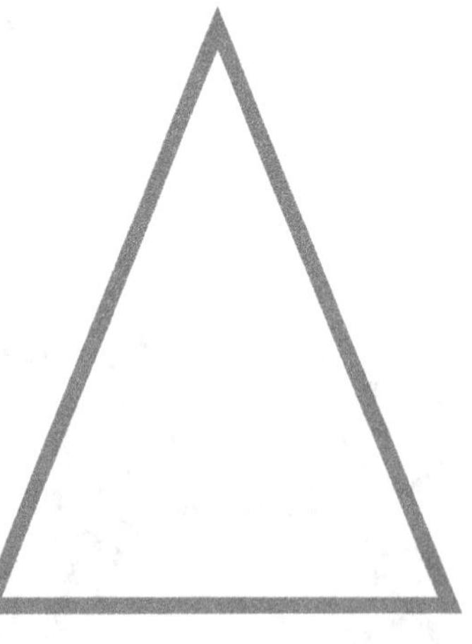

WOULD YOU RATHER......

Be able to master origami

-OR-

Hand magic

WOULD YOU RATHER......

Eat a dish of spaghetti

-OR-

Eat a piece of steak

WOULD YOU RATHER......

Be able to survive falls from any height

-OR-

Be bulletproof

WOULD YOU RATHER......

Eat brocoli flavored ice cream

-OR-

Meat flavored cookies

WOULD YOU RATHER......

Be able to master origami

-OR-

Hand magic

WOULD YOU RATHER……

Have super speed

-OR-

Super strength

WOULD YOU RATHER......

Become a dancer

-OR-

Become an engineer

WOULD YOU RATHER......

Wear trendy sneakers

-OR-

Wear cute shoes

WOULD YOU RATHER......

Live in a cave

-OR-

A tree house

WOULD YOU RATHER......

Meet an alien

~OR~

Meet a god

WOULD YOU RATHER......

Play games on a phone

-OR-

Play a board game

WOULD YOU RATHER......

Go to a

<u>Tea</u> -OR- <u>Costume</u>

Party

WOULD YOU RATHER......

Raise chickens

Raise cows

WOULD YOU RATHER......

See a giant ant

-OR-

A tiny giraffe

WOULD YOU RATHER......

Play paint ball

-OR-

Laser tag

WOULD YOU RATHER......

Speak every language

-OR-

Play every instrument

WOULD YOU RATHER......

Eat

<u>Oatmeal</u>   <u>Cereal</u>

-OR-

WOULD YOU RATHER......

Watch videos online

-OR-

On television

WOULD YOU RATHER......

Be a ninja

Be a spy

WOULD YOU RATHER......

Live with your grandma

-OR-

Live with your cousins

WOULD YOU

YOU

RATHER......

Eat

Milk -OR- _Dark_

Chocolate

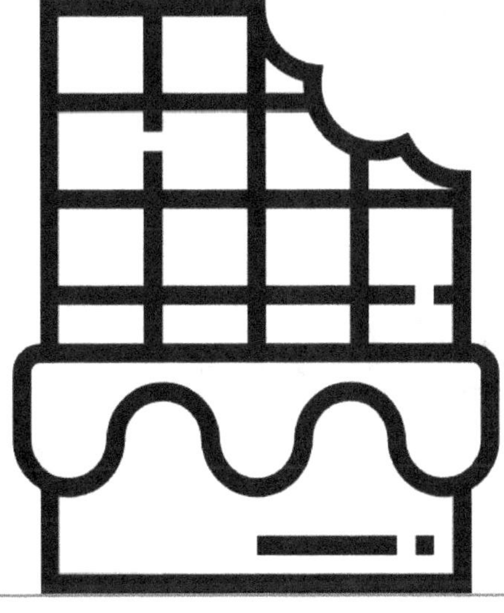

WOULD YOU RATHER......

Clean up your

Bathroom

-OR-

Bedroom

WOULD YOU RATHER......

Eat bread with butter

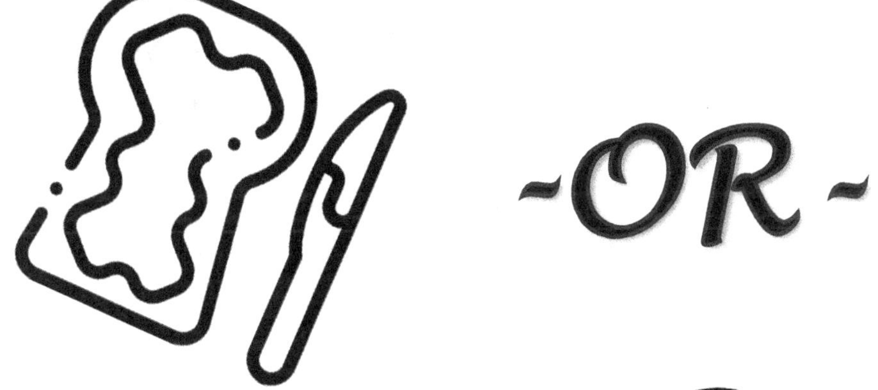

-OR-

With jam

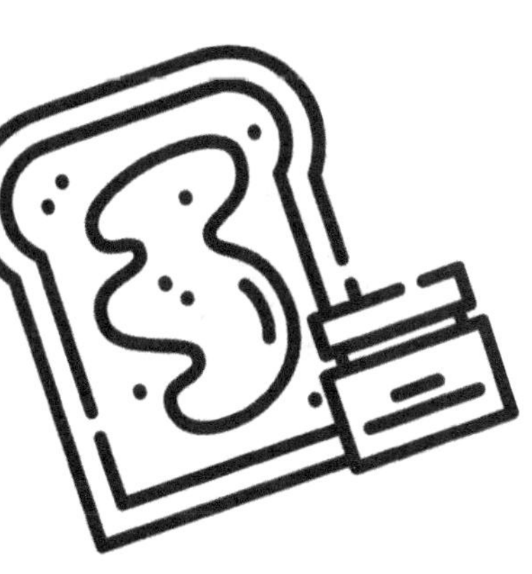

WOULD YOU RATHER......

Eat chips with ketchup 

-OR-

With mustard

WOULD YOU RATHER......

Take the stairs

-OR-

The elevator

WOULD YOU RATHER......

Live in a house made of gummy bears

-OR-

Marshmallows

WOULD YOU RATHER......

Be an Olympic athlete

-OR-

The President

WOULD YOU RATHER......

Constantly itch

-OR-

Always have
a cough